The Gutsy Girls of Science

First published in India in 2022 by HarperCollins Children's Books
An imprint of HarperCollins *Publishers*
Building no 10, Tower A, 4th floor, DLF Cyber City,
Phase II, Gurugram 122002, India
www.harpercollins.co.in

2 4 6 8 10 9 7 5 3 1

P-ISBN: 978-93-5489-596-8
E-ISBN: 978-93-5489-272-1

Cover illustration: Ilina Singh
Design and layout: Naveen Kumar

Typeset in Merriweather 10pt/19

Printed and bound at
Lustra Print Process Pvt. Ltd.

HarperCollinsIn

The Gutsy Girls of Science

WRITTEN AND ILLUSTRATED
BY ILINA SINGH

HarperCollinsChildren'sBooks

Foreword by

Eric Falt

With intelligence and an innate artistic talent, young Ilina Singh presents through this book 11 trailblazing Indian women who overcame all odds to achieve success in Science, Technology, Engineering and Mathematics (STEM). Well researched and sharply written, this book introduces the careers of these role models, who represent various scientific disciplines and various parts of India. Among the pages of this book, you will meet cytogeneticist Archana Sharma; botanist Janaki Ammal, mathematician Raman Parimala; physicist Bibha Chowdhuri; chemist Asima Chatterjee; and many others.

Ilina has showed her admiration for these achievers in the form of poems and colorful illustrations, telling each woman's story with engaging artwork, poetic tributes and fun facts. She interweaved touching personal anecdotes, resulting in a pleasant and inquisitive narrative. The book is also packed with fascinating information about science and experiments to encourage critical thinking.

UNESCO, for its part, is keen to reinforce its commitment to the 2030 Agenda for Sustainable Development. At present, less than 30 per cent of researchers worldwide are women, and only 30 per cent of all female students select STEM-related fields in higher education. Globally, female students' enrolment is particularly low in information and communications technology (3 per cent), natural science, mathematics and statistics (5 per cent) and in engineering, manufacturing and construction (8 per cent).

UNESCO considers it more vital than ever to promote equality throughout the education system, to transform unequal power relations by challenging gender stereotypes and norms, and to showcase strong role models for women in STEM.

Ilina's fascinating book will surely encourage young female readers to imagine themselves as the gutsy women scientists of the future, and will invite young men to know better and to admire these extraordinary 11 Indian women scientists.

Eric Falt

Director and UNESCO Representative to
Bhutan, India, Maldives and Sri Lanka

Contents

For

Gutsy Girls everywhere

and

especially for Nani

Archana Sharma

(1932–2008)

Cytogeneticist

Cytogenetics, now that's a word
that sounds rather weighty.
It won Archana a Padma Bhushan
in the decade of eighty.

Just as a house that's fine
is made of the humble brick.
In your body and mine
it's the cell that does the trick.

Deep inside each cell there roams
a set of human chromosomes.
These molecules are rather long
and are the music to your life's song.

Deciding whether you'll be healthy or sick,
creating cacophony or sweet music.
Archana knew this well and
was the conductor of this merry band!

Dr. Archana Sharma was a renowned Indian botanist. She published 400 research papers and 8 books. In 1984, Archana was awarded one of India's highest national honours – the Padma Bhushan.

This was a culmination of a long and illustrious journey that began several years earlier.

Archana was born in 1932 in Pune. Her father N.P. Mukherjee was a chemistry professor in Bikaner and consequently Archana too did her graduation in Bikaner. She then moved to Calcutta University where she ended up spending a considerable amount of time. She completed her M.Sc, PhD and DSc from the university. Archana was the second woman scientist to be awarded the DSc from Calcutta University in 1960. She continued her association by joining the genetics department of the university in 1967 and remained there until her retirement.

In 1955, Archana married Arun Kumar Sharma, himself a botanist of repute, and together they collaborated on many research projects, including publishing a book - 'Chromosome Techniques: Theory and Practice'- considered a standard reference book in the field.

Archana's scientific research cut across various fields.

- She studied polymorphism and its correlation to diseases in humans.
- She conducted research on the impact of pesticides on cells.
- Archana, along with her team, did significant work on understanding the effect of arsenic in water.
- She worked on the cytotaxonomy of flowering plants. One of her major discoveries was the concept of speciation in vegetatively reproducing plants.
- She did cutting-edge work in studying the structure of chromosomes, developing a new staining and pre-treatment technique.

Archana's contribution to the field of botany went beyond her own personal research. In 1972, a few years after she had joined Calcutta University, she became the Professor of Genetics in the Centre for Advanced Studies in Cell and Chromosome Research.
In 1981, she became the head of the Department of Botany.
She was considered an excellent teacher who trained many bright researchers who went on to make a significant impact in the field.

She was also on various committees of UGC and DST. She was a member of various professional societies such as the Indian Academy of Science and the National Academy of Science among others and held key positions in them. She was Secretary General and later President of the Indian Science Congress Association.

For her stellar work in botany, cytogenetics and cytotoxicology, Dr. Archana Sharma was awarded the highest science award of India – the Shanti Swaroop Bhatnagar Award – in 1976.

Not only is Archana remembered for her amazing work in the field of botany but she also garnered a huge amount of praise and affection from her peers and students as a person. The Alumni association of the PG Department of Botany at the Calcutta University issued a special publication in her honour in which students and colleagues wrote with great fondness about the memories of "Archana Di".

India is fortunate to have had a scientific mind like Dr. Archana Sharma. Her contribution as a researcher, a teacher and a mentor has left an indelible mark on the field of botany and cytogenetics.

So, you want to be a Cytogeneticist

Cytogenetics is a relatively new field of science – it wasn't till the 1960s that medical practice started studying genetics and the role of chromosomes seriously.

The trigger for this was the discovery that Down's Syndrome was caused by a defect in the chromosome. Prenatal diagnosis of genetic disorders became an immediate area of interest. With technological advances, it has been possible to study human genetic variations at the level of the DNA.

This has opened a fascinating field of medicine where disease associated with abnormal chromosomes can be diagnosed early.

Activity

Here is a puzzle for you to solve. Do look up the meaning of all these words that are common in the world of cytogenetics. If this awakens your curiosity, do follow up with more exploration of this fascinating field.

Cytogenetic Puzzle

H	E	T	G	S	I	M	I	O	E	S	R	T	S
E	A	N	O	I	T	A	T	U	M	G	I	E	T
S	I	N	I	O	E	C	E	N	S	N	T	X	M
Y	E	R	I	S	O	E	H	M	C	I	M	P	I
A	C	H	C	I	V	Y	G	T	P	P	M	R	T
N	C	A	N	C	E	R	M	O	H	Y	Y	E	O
D	O	N	I	P	I	E	X	O	E	T	S	S	S
T	A	I	S	D	I	T	R	O	N	O	O	S	I
T	X	N	H	O	S	A	T	R	O	Y	S	I	S
N	O	S	S	N	N	N	O	S	T	R	E	V	G
H	D	I	P	O	N	S	M	M	Y	A	R	I	E
U	S	S	C	E	I	H	Y	M	P	K	G	T	N
X	O	E	R	I	N	I	O	R	E	R	V	Y	E
T	A	C	H	R	O	M	O	S	O	M	E	I	C

MEIOSIS
CHROMOSOME
KARYOTYPING
CANCER
EXPRESSIVITY
MITOSIS
MUTATION
GENE
PHENOTYPE
DNA

Janaki Ammal

(1897-1984)

Botanist

There was something about Janaki,
that made her
the Queen of Botany.

She made
Indian sugar sweeter,
and gave Kerala's Silent Valley a breather.

A scientist very bright, she evokes such pride.
From her are the
names of two flowers derived!

When you add a spoon of sugar to your milk tomorrow, you can smile and say a silent thanks to Janaki.

Who is Janaki, you may well ask!

Let's begin at the beginning.

The year was 1897. A baby girl was born in the house of a judge in Thalassery in Kerala. She was the 10th of 19 children born in this family. She was given the name Edavaleth Kakkat Janaki Ammal. Janaki's father kept a garden and wrote books on the birds of the North Malabar region. It was no surprise, then, that little Janaki developed an early interest in natural sciences and plants that only deepened as she grew up. Janaki's elder sisters had arranged marriages, as was the custom at the time. However, when her turn came and a match was being arranged for her, she chose to pursue higher studies in botany. This was quite unusual for a girl in those days. India was still ruled by the British.

Less than one out of 100 Indian women were literate. Fewer than 1000 girls were enrolled in school above 10th grade. Janaki was taking a road less travelled.

She went on to teach botany for three years at the Women's Christian College, Madras, before being invited to the University of Michigan on a scholarship. In Michigan, she worked on plant cytology – the composition of plant genes and their expression. She went on to do her M.Sc and then became the first Indian woman to become a doctorate in botany from the USA. She spent many years working in London. Here, she met her longtime mentor and collaborator C D. Darlington with whom she co–authored the book 'Chromosome Atlas of Cultivated Plants' in 1945.

Her next stop was as a cytologist at the Royal Horticultural Society, Wesley, where she studied the Magnolia plant and conducted experiments on its hybridization.

When India became free, the country needed good botanists and Janaki was invited by India's first Prime Minister, Jawaharlal Nehru, to run the Botanical Survey of India (BSI) and was appointed its Director-General.

So, what's her connection to the sugar in your milk?
Did you know that the Indian variety of sugarcane was not the best either in sweetness or in yield? In fact, India used to import the sweetest sugarcanes from other countries. The Indian Sugarcane Breeding Station at Coimbatore invited Janaki for her help since she was an expert. She managed to create a hybrid variety of sugarcane in her lab that had higher sweetness and could do well in Indian climatic conditions. In later years, she worked hard to preserve India's environment and local breeds of plants. She was key in influencing decision-makers to cancel the plan to build a dam in Kerala. This dam would have caused Kerala's Silent Valley habitats to be flooded with water.

Janaki's work was celebrated and valued in India. She was awarded the Padma Shri in 1977. The Ministry of Environment and Forestry created the National Award of Taxonomy in her name in 2000. The Janaki Ammal Herbarium in Jammu is also a tribute to her. The Indian government established the Janaki Ammal National Women Bioscientist Award.

In 2020, she was one of 11 women scientists who were honoured by the Ministries of Women and Child Development and Science and Technology ahead of Women's Day.

A chair was set up with a grant of up to Rupees one crore for researchers for their projects with the intention of encouraging and inspiring young girls interested in pursuing the study of science.

Most appropriately, she has three species of plants named after her – a herb, a rose and her favourite magnolias.

Herb **Magnolias** **Rose**

Would you like to be a Botanist

Well, let's try to answer that by first finding out what exactly botanists do and why it is of use to the world.

Botany is the science that studies plants. It's a subset of Biology which is the science of studying all living things.

If you look around, you'll quickly understand the importance of plants in our lives. The food we eat, the air we breathe, the environment we live in and the objects we use to construct much of our world – plants impact every aspect of human life.

Activity

To understand what exactly a botanist does, and how she makes a difference to the world, here's something you could do.

01 List a couple of famous botanists you might have heard of. You can ask a teacher or check online for suggestions if you like.

02 Try to read up as much about them as you can and then organize your learning along these five headings: When, what, where, how and why.

03 When did they live and work? What was the focus of their work? Where did they live and work? How did they contribute to the field of botany? Why do you feel their work made our world better?

04 Next, try to make two tables, one which summarizes as many similarities in the botanists as you can think of and the other citing their differences.

You could study more botanists over time. This will give you a better idea of what botanists do and how they can impact the world. You can then make an informed choice on whether you'd like to study botany further.

Darshan Ranganathan

(1941–2001)

Organic Chemistry

When the cards are folded and put away
and the light fades at the end of the day,
how many can look back happily and say,
I did what I wanted and
I did it my way.

Was Darshan a bright star, nay a comet?
That's how her loving husband later saw it.
Blazing across the horizon of chemistry,
how she accomplished
so much is a mystery.

She challenged the glass ceiling with resolve
and marched on as she saw obstacles dissolve.
She did so with elegance, panache and style,
wearing her silk sarees and
her dazzling smile!

Jackfruit is considered a delicious fruit by many Indians.

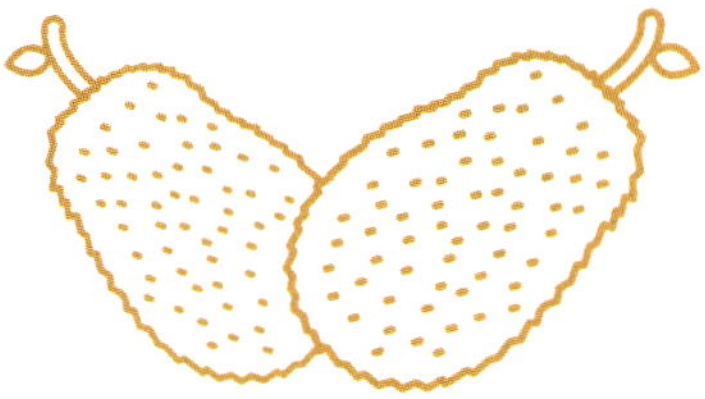

So, while it isn't surprising to hear that Darshan asked her mother for this fruit, it is amazing that she made this request while she lived in faraway London! And what is even more unusual is that she did not want to eat the South Asian delicacy, but to clarify the structure of cycloartenol – a plant-based chemical found in jackfruit.

Once you realize the level of commitment and dedication that Darshan had for studying biochemistry, the stellar success of Darshan's work in the field comes as no surprise. What's also easy to understand is the inquisitive nature of this researcher, which probably played a big part in her ability to secure research fellowships during her entire career. This is no small feat today, but it was very rare when Darshan started working. Darshan's journey began in Delhi in 1941. She was born to the family of Shantiswarup and Vidyavati Makan, in Karol Bagh. During her schooling, she decided to pursue chemistry. She continued her studies in Delhi University, eventually completing her PhD in organic chemistry. Whilst completing her PhD, she also taught

at Miranda House College in Delhi.

She then went on to the Imperial College in London, to work on her post-doctoral research. It was while doing this research on cycloartenol, that the need to study the bio-chemical in jackfruit arose, leading to her request to her mother to send her the jackfruit in dried form from Delhi to London. Her passion and innovative solution helped her professor complete his research. Darshan focused on studying the structures of organic compounds and the field of protein folding. She has done pioneering work on the protocol for autonomous reproduction of imidazole. This had a significant impact on the field of pharmaceuticals – specifically, antibiotics and antifungal drugs.

On returning to India, she married a fellow scientist and researcher – Subramania Ranganathan and moved to IIT Kanpur with her husband.

She continued her work which led to her being recognized as a leading organic biochemist in India.

She was a member of the Indian Academy of Sciences and published multiple papers. She moved to the Regional Research Laboratory in Trivandrum in 1992. In 1998, she and her husband were invited to the Indian Institute of Chemical Technology in Hyderabad and moved there together.

Sadly, she was diagnosed with cancer and passed away in 2001, but not before she had left an indelible mark on the field of biochemistry.

So, you want to study Organic Chemistry

Well that's great, because organic chemistry is something totally unique.

It's the branch of chemistry that studies compounds containing carbon.

Did you know that life on earth is also referred to as carbon-based life? Why? Because all life is based on carbon-based compounds. Have you heard of hydrocarbons?

The petrol that we put in the car is comprised of hydrocarbons. Do you know where these come from? Well, they originate from biological matter which is hundreds of millions of years old. So, when you study organic chemistry you truly understand how the mighty T–Rex from the Jurassic age finally decomposes to become something that we fill in the petrol tank of a car. Interesting enough?

Activity

Organic Chemistry Card Game

So, what are we doing here? We're making organic molecules.

Let's try to see how molecules are made by creating some ourselves. Your molecules may or may not be found in nature. Don't worry, even if they are not real, they will be quite close to what's found naturally.

Here is the alphabet key: H=hydrogen, C=carbon, O=oxygen, N=nitrogen, Cl=chlorine, Br=bromine, F=fluorine.

Notice how many hydrogen cards there are in the game. Nearly 90% of all atoms in the universe are hydrogen! The lines on the cards represent electrons that the atom would like to share with another atom.

Instructions

01 Give each player 5 cards. The rest go into a draw pile. Put one of the carbons (with no double bonds) face up as the starter card.

02 The players take turns laying down cards, trying to get rid of all their cards. The first player to get rid of all the cards wins. HOWEVER, the last card he lays down MUST complete a molecule in order to win the game. If a player lays down his last card on an incomplete molecule, he must then draw another card. He may not lay down this new card immediately but must wait until his next turn to play it. The lines represent bonds. A player must match single bonds to single bonds and double bonds to double bonds. The molecule is complete when no bonds are "left hanging." Each bond (line) must have an atom attached to it.

03 Notice that there are dotted lines on the double bond O. This is so you can turn the card caddy-corner and match the double bond with two single bonds.

04 If a player cannot lay down a card, he must take one from the draw pile. He may lay down this card immediately if he can do so. If a molecule is finished and all players are still holding cards, simply begin another molecule. Remember, you must use a single bond carbon (four lines) to begin a new molecule.

05 To win the game, a player must lay down his last card as the final atom in a molecule.

Scan the QR code to print the cards and cut out the squares along the dotted lines to make your game cards.
This game can be played by 2-6 players.

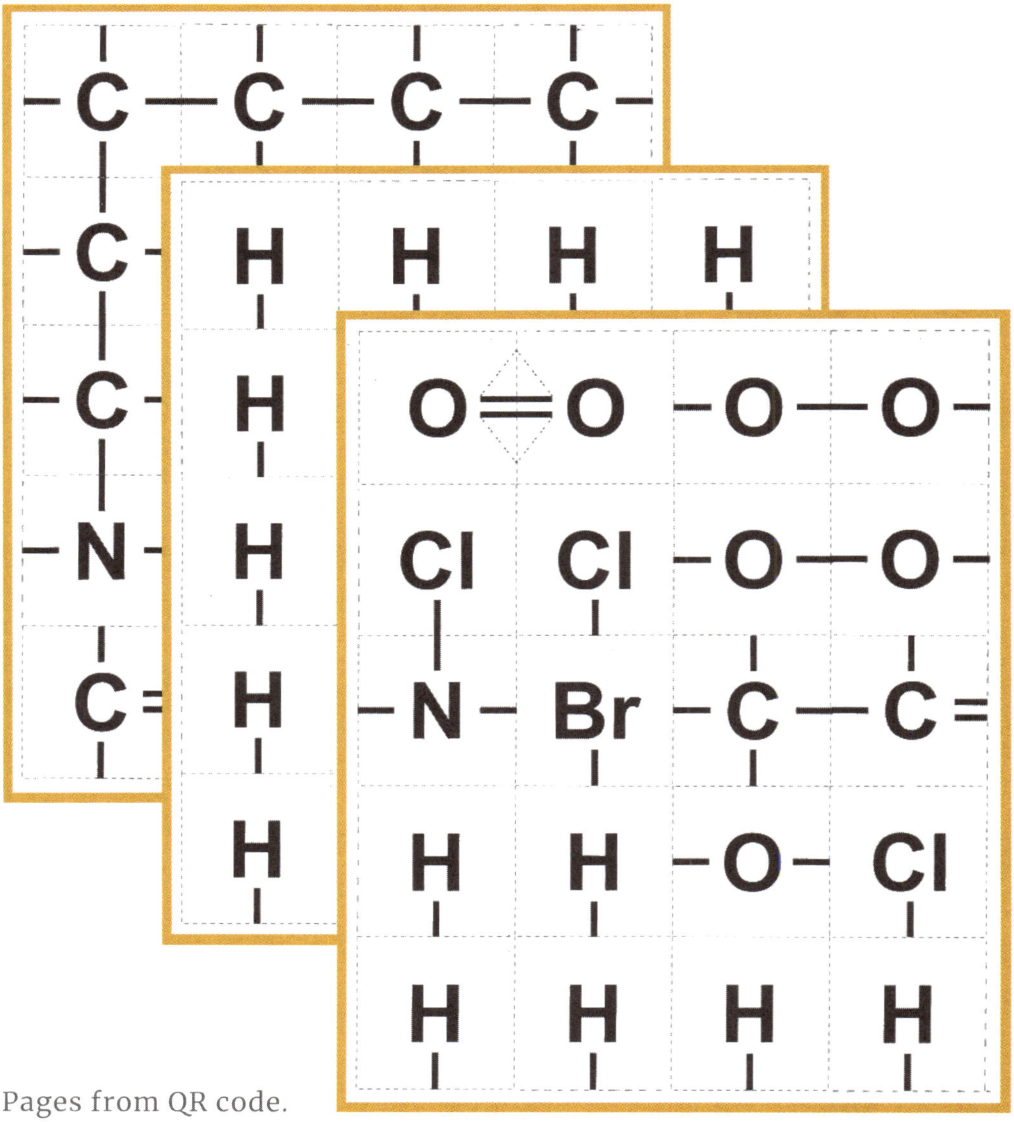

Pages from QR code.

Asima Chatterjee

(1917–2006)

Chemist

A girl set out to study an organic compound,
ignoring naysayers, she was on solid ground.

She discovered the medicine for an illness pesky,
Eureka, Ayush 56 was the cure for epilepsy.

Chemotherapy and anti-malaria drugs came next,
the country applauded as her research skills she flexed.

When asked, how much could she possibly give:
She replied, "I wish to work as long as I live."

We could go on and on, but we must confess,
Asima, true to her name, was limitless!

On September 23, 1917, Dr. Indra Narayan Mukherjee and his wife Kamala Devi welcomed their first-born child—a baby girl—into their home in Calcutta, West Bengal. The girl was named Asima.

Theirs was a middle-class family which placed high value on education. Asima was encouraged to study well, even though it was rare in those days for women to get proper academic exposure. Her father loved botany and Asima too developed an interest in the subject. As we will see later, plants did play a very important role in her life's work. Her choice of subject for higher studies was chemistry.

She graduated with honours from Scottish Church College in 1936 and got her Master's degree in 1938. She became the founding head of the Department of Chemistry at Lady Brabourne College.

She went on to complete her doctoral degree in 1944 in organic chemistry.

This made her the first Indian woman with a doctorate in science.

Later, she went on to get research experience from the University of Wisconsin, Madison and Caltech. In the year 1945, Asima got married to another chemist – Dr. Baradananda Chatterjee. Her daughter Julie was born soon after. Her husband went on to become the Professor and Head of the Department of Chemistry, Geology and Metallurgy at the Bengal Engineering College, Howrah.

Dr. Asima now juggled domestic and work responsibilities with aplomb as she made great strides in her research. Her husband was supportive of her professional life and sometimes even helped her research students when he visited her at work.

Her students recall the lack of resources and facilities that often came up as obstacles in her work. Indian science was not too well funded, and she sometimes had to pay from her personal budget to get samples tested abroad. She often did not have money to pay the salaries of her students. They had to use old instruments to derive tiny amounts of active compounds from plants. Still, she diligently ploughed through the tough circumstances and made great progress in medicinal chemistry. She wrote around 400 papers in national and international journals. Her work has been cited widely and is part of textbooks.

In her 40-year career, she developed several drugs that were used to treat epilepsy and malaria and others that were used in chemotherapy.

The anti-epilepsy drug Ayush-56, discovered by her, is still used. She also wrote many books in English and Bengali.

Dr. Asima was a rare example of an Indian woman scientist who got the recognition due to her in her lifetime. She won several awards like the S S Bhatnagar Award, the C V Raman Award, and the P C Ray Award; and was awarded the Padma Bhushan, the third-highest civilian award, in recognition of her contributions to science. She was also the first woman to be elected as the General President of the Indian Science Congress.

She presented a great example of the much-desired work-life balance. She enjoyed cooking, spending time with her family and the simple joys of family life. She worked till the end of her life. She passed away peacefully at the age of 90. Her daughter followed in her footsteps and became a chemist too.

So, you want to study Chemistry

Great! Do you know what's the building block of chemistry?

Well, it's all the elements in the universe! From the lightest one Hydrogen—which is the most abundant element in the universe—to Polonium, a rare and highly radioactive element.

Humans have been studying elements for a long time. Copper, silver, gold, iron were part of early human settlements. But not all elements were known in those ancient times. We keep discovering new elements all the time. In fact, now scientists create new elements! To name a few: Einsteinium (named after Albert Einstein), Curium (named after Marie Curie) and Mendelevium 101 (named after Dimitri Mendeleev, the father of the periodic table).

Who knows, once you become a famous scientist, maybe there could be an element named after you. Would you like that? But if it's an element like the three named above, then I suggest you don't try to keep a memento made out of it at your home – because each of these is radioactive!

Activity

Acidic or Basic? Let's find out.

Have you ever wondered about the chemical nature of your household items?
There are strips of paper, named pH paper, that can reveal exactly that. When you dip the paper in a solution, the substance in the paper causes the paper to show a different colour at different levels of acidity.

The official pH scale is from 0 to 6, where 0 is very acidic and 6 very alkaline.

The image given below shows the colours the scale would display in relation to certain liquids.

The pH Scale

Select any 5 liquids and test them using the pH paper. Write down your observation in the table given below, as well as what number on the pH scale you think the solution is.

Liquid Number	Name of Liquid	Colour	pH Number

Kadambini Ganguly

(1861–1923)

Physician

What's one to do when one finds a closed door?
Why, one can knock on it, unlock it, or even more ...
One can sometimes break it down
like young Kadambini did!

**She didn't take no for an answer,
didn't care who forbid.
When she dreamt of becoming
one of India's first physicians,
those-in-charge reacted with shock,
derision and suspicion.**

Proving them wrong, she sailed through with aplomb,
managing work and eight kids with a smile and a song.

On July 18, 1861, baby Kadambini was born in the house of Braja Kishore Basu, a Brahmo Samaj reformer. Her family lived in Bhagalpur, Bihar in British India where her father was the headmaster of the Bhagalpur School. They hailed from Chandsi in present day Bangladesh. The atmosphere at home was conducive to academics and the empowerment of women. In 1863, Braja Kishore, along with other like-minded people, started the first women's organization in India – the Bhagalpur Mahila Samiti. With the wholehearted support of her father, Kadambini started a life of scholarly pursuit which would lead her to accomplish dreams that were deemed impossible for women of her time.

After receiving her initial education at the Banga Mahila Vidyalya, she went to the Bethune School in 1878. She became the first woman to pass the University of Calcutta's entrance exam.

She worked for the progress of women and lobbied along with others for the introduction of FA (Fine Arts), and graduation courses at the Bethune College. Kadambini and a fellow woman scholar were not just the first graduates from Bethune College, but also the first female graduates in India and indeed, the British Empire.

This was just a steppingstone in her ambitious journey. She decided to join a medical college next. The Calcutta Medical College did not allow women so Kadambini had to put up a struggle to be allowed in. She enrolled in the college in 1884 after crossing the many obstacles put up by the college and even received a scholarship from the government.

Around this time, Kadambini married Dwarakanath Ganguly, a prominent Brahmo reformer. They went on to have a large family of eight children. Dwarakanath was also very progressive in his views and was both a mentor and a strong supporter of Kadambini's professional aspirations. The marriage was successful even though there was opposition from society due to the large age difference between them.

In 1886, she was awarded GBMC and became the first woman physician with a Western medical degree in South Asia.

After her graduation, she joined the Lady Dufferin Women's Hospital (where her salary was Rs. 200 per month) for a short stint before deciding to sail to London in 1892 for further education.

This move stemmed partly from the stiff resistance she faced from her colleagues who could not come to terms with a woman joining their ranks. She qualified as LRCP (Edinburgh), LRCS (Glasgow) and GFPS (Dublin) before returning to India and practicing as a doctor.

She went on to have a very successful career as a doctor for 37 years until her death in 1923 at the age of 62. It is important to mention that she led a rich and accomplished personal and public life as well. She was a nationalist and an activist for women's rights. She worked to organize meetings expressing support for Satyagraha and opposing the British rule in India. She was also known for her embroidery and lace-making skills.

Kadambini was a trailblazer who defeated all odds to prove that women can have a brilliant career in STEM.

So, you want to be a Doctor

That's awesome! Doctors and medical professionals really make a huge impact on our lives. Do you know some of the most famous doctors? Let me tell you about a few.

Well, there was the Hippocrates in ancient Greece, considered the father of medicine. In ancient India, there was Charaka, considered the father of the Indian Ayurvedic medicine system. In more modern times there was Edward Jenner, the 18th century doctor who found the cure for smallpox. Alexander Fleming discovered penicillin, the first antibiotic. Virginia Apgar, an American doctor invented the 'Apgar Score', a way to quickly assess the health of a newborn child. And there was Christian Barnard, who performed the first human-to-human heart transplant.
Do these names inspire you to do something stellar in the field of medicine? I'm sure they will.

Activity

Physicians often check a patient's pulse rate during physical examinations. Let's learn how to check your pulse.

You can easily check your pulse on the inside of your wrist, below your thumb. Gently place two fingers of your other hand on this artery. Do not use your thumb because it has its own pulse that you may feel.

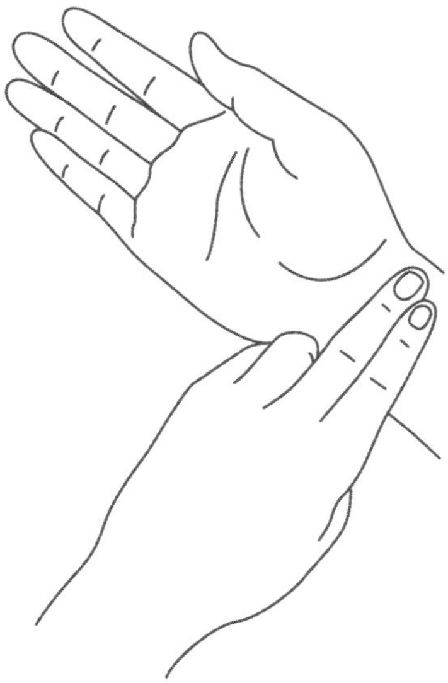

Now measure your pulse for ten seconds according to the activity the table lists and fill it out.

Find out what happens to your heart rate when you do physical activities!

Heart rates are calculated in beats per minute (bpm). Your regular resting heart rate (when you are not doing any physical activities) should range between 60 and 100bpm.

Use this table to calculate your heart rate:

	Beats in 10 seconds	Multiply by 6	Beats per minute
Resting		x 6	
Jogging		x 6	
Jumping Jacks		x 6	
Resting		x 6	

Write down your observation. What do you think this means? Write down your inferences. Read up on what an elevated or slow pulse rate could mean when a patient has not been physically exerting himself.

Iravati Karve

(1905–1970)

Anthropologist

As discovered by the young Iravati,
the long word Anthropology –
Meant the study of humanity
its customs, beliefs and society.

She researched these for our country,
and earned our respect for eternity.

On December 15, 1905, Ganesh Hari Karmarkar, a wealthy and well-educated Indian engineer working for the Burma Cotton Company, welcomed the arrival of his baby daughter. He named his daughter after the largest river in Burma – the Irrawaddy. This was perhaps a sign of his global outlook and as we shall see, Iravati gained international fame with her work.

The family prized education and Iravati was sent to a boarding school in Pune at the age of seven. She studied philosophy at Fergusson College and completed her graduation in 1926. She was a bright student. After she was awarded the Dakshina Fellowship by the Maharashtra government, she studied sociology at the University of Bombay where she met her mentor GS Ghurye. He proved to be a great guide and influenced her thinking and academic development. Her thesis topic was inspired by her own caste and was titled 'The Chitpavan Brahmans – An Ethnic Study'. She completed her Master's in 1928.

On the personal front too Iravati was an independent thinker. While her father had hoped that she would marry royalty, she chose a chemistry teacher named Dinkar Dhondo Karve as her husband. He came from a distinguished family and Iravati's father-in-law, Dhondo Keshav Karve, was actively involved in promoting women's education. She travelled to Germany to complete her MPhil in anthropology from the University of Berlin in 1930. She was quite ahead of her times in her thinking and behaviour. She was one of the first women two-wheeler drivers of Pune in 1952 and liked to drive around town when it was quite uncommon for a woman to do so alone.

Her views on women's rights can be summarized by the following quote:

"Ladies, while fighting with men for rights, why fight for only equal rights always fight for more rights."

One of the most impactful contributions she made to her chosen subject was the creation of the Anthropology Department at Poona (now Pune) University.
Indology, or the study of Indian history, literature, philosophy, and culture, was one of the central themes running through her work. She presented a non-anglicized view of India's culture and heritage. She quietly challenged the prevalent colonial narrative that emphasized the differences in Indian people by illuminating the threads of unity in the diversity.

Her interest in the kinship structures in Indian society made her examine the language dialects and geographical patterns across regions. Her findings were published under the title 'Kinship Organization in India'. She did this at a time when it was rare for a woman to take up anthropology due to the travel to remote regions as well as the physically taxing nature of the work. However, she was able to establish herself early as a renowned expert in the subject and her publications were often studied and quoted in the national and international arena.

Several achievements and accolades came Iravati's way. She headed the Departments of Sociology and Anthropology at Deccan College, Pune for forty years. She was also appointed the Vice-Chancellor of SNDT College. She presided over the Anthropology Division of the National Science Congress held in New Delhi in 1947.

Dr. Karve wrote the book 'Yuganta' for which she received the Sahitya Academy Award in 1968.

Would you like to be an Anthropologist

Let’s begin at the very beginning to see whether you might like to take up this science as a career. Why do we need anthropologists and why is their work valuable?

Anthropology, quite simply, is the “science of humanity”.

It is a broad term that contains specialized subjects like evolutionary history of Homo Sapiens, biology and aspects of culture and society that differentiate us from other species. Its importance as a science continues as the world gets more interconnected and we need to understand different cultures to build bridges and overcome differences. Also, of all the sciences, this one has the power to influence policy and public opinion.

Activity

Did you know that you, like everyone else, are part of a unique family tree? When your maternal and paternal grandparents had children, a new branch was added to their family trees. Guess who is the freshest branch on the tree? Yes, it's you.

You could paste photos of your family in the circles and write their names in the boxes. And then cut it out and pin it to your wall.
How would the tree look if all the siblings were counted too? Can you tell the names of your great grandparents?

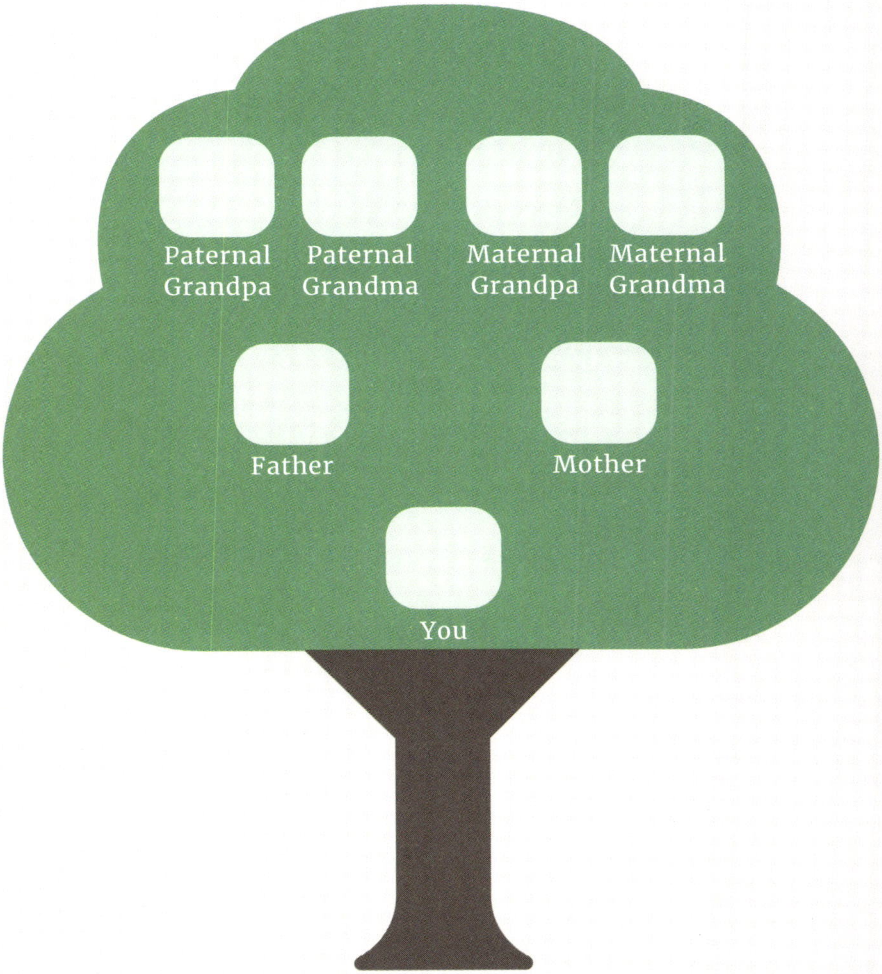

Anna Mani

(1918–2001)

Meteorologist

Want to know whether it will be cloudy or sunny?

Well, you should perhaps first thank Anna Mani,
a physicist who studied the diamond and the ruby.
Who soon shifted gears to welcome what was meant to be,
a future as the leading light in Indian meteorology –
– wind speed, solar energy and that gas called Ozone.

She was a pioneer and made the unknown known!

Anna Mani was born in 1918 at Peermade, Kerala into the family of an affluent civil engineer. Her father owned large cardamom estates and encouraged his sons to study science and do well academically. As was the custom in those times, even well-educated families did not expect their daughters to pursue a career, and young Anna was groomed to marry instead of excelling at academics like her brothers.

However, Anna had a mind of her own. She took advantage of the academic atmosphere at home and was a voracious reader. She had finished reading all the Malayalam books in her library by the age of eight and then went on to read all the English books available by the age of twelve. She loved books so much that as the story goes, when she was gifted diamond earrings at the age of eight, she declined the gift and requested for a copy of the Encyclopedia Britannica instead.

In 1939, she received her B.Sc Honours degree in physics and chemistry from the Pachaiyappas College in Madras. She was a bright student and won a scholarship for research at the prestigious Indian Institute of Science, Bangalore in 1940.

Here, she decided to focus on physics and started her research on the spectroscopy of diamonds and rubies. She was supervised by the Nobel Laureate Sir C.V. Raman. She submitted five research papers and a PhD dissertation but since she did not have a Master's degree, she was not given a PhD despite the detailed research work. However, she did not let this setback affect her. When she was offered a scholarship to study physics at the Imperial College, London for her research work, she grabbed the opportunity. She sailed for London in 1945 on a troop ship with the intent of continuing her pursuit of physics. However, when she found out that the only internship available was in meteorological instrumentation, she decided to switch subjects. This was one of those twists of fate that helped Anna stand out in a field that was developing in India.

On her return to India in 1948, Anna accepted a position at the India Meteorological Department in Pune. Here, her first task was to standardize the drawings of the instruments used in the measurement of weather. Drawing standards for more than 100 such instruments were created. Next, she worked on tapping solar energy by setting up monitoring stations across India to measure solar radiation. She also supervised the design and development of many instruments that measured radiation. Mani headed a project at IMD to design weather instruments.

She is credited with ensuring the development of instruments that measured weather phenomena accurately.

She believed that "wrong measurements are worse than no measurements at all."

In 1960, Mani started an interesting project – the measurement of atmospheric ozone. She went on to develop an instrument to measure ozone and became a member of the International Ozone Association.

Anna also worked to have a meteorological observatory set up at the Thumba rocket launching facility. An instrumentation tower was also added. In 1976, she retired as deputy director general of the IMD. She took up the position of visiting professor to the Raman Research Institute, Bengaluru. Here too, she set up a facility with a millimetre-wave telescope at Nandi Hills.

Anna was known for her strong work ethic. She chose not to get married and was totally dedicated to her career, academic pursuits and service to the nation. She was a nature lover and enjoyed trekking and bird watching. She was very impressed by Gandhian thought and wore khadi clothes for most of her life.

She was a member of many scientific organizations – the Indian National Science Academy, the American Meteorological Society and the International Solar Energy Society to name a few.

She authored two definitive books that still serve as references for budding scientists – 'Handbook of Solar Radiation Data for India' and 'Solar Radiation over India'.

Later, the prolific Mani also started a company that made precision instruments to measure solar radiation and wind speed. Her work on projects to measure wind speeds across India was the precursor to India harnessing wind energy.

In 1987, she received the INSA K. R. Ramanathan Medal for her achievements. In 1994, she suffered a stroke and passed away on August 16, 2001 in Thiruvananthapuram.

Would you like to be a Meteorologist

Meteorologists are scientists who study weather and climate.

Humans have tried to predict the weather since ancient times since our survival as farmers depended on it. The scientific study of weather started much later, and the accuracy of our predictions has gone up over time. When you want to know whether you can plan a picnic on Sunday, you rely on the work of these scientists. Their work helps save lives as they give advance warnings of floods and other natural disasters.

Activity

Let's make a wind vane.

There was a time when knowing the direction of the wind was very important to predict whether a storm was brewing. However, now these are mainly of decorative interest.

Materials

- Clay or play dough
- Square cardboard base
- Pencil with rubber eraser
- Pin
- Straw
- Scissors
- Colourful art/kite paper
- Markers or crayons
- Compass

Instructions

01) Using the compass, identify North. Then, write North, South, East, and West on a square piece of cardboard.

02) Cut a notch into each end of the straw.

03) Cut an arrow and a tail out of construction paper, then slip them into the slits on the straw.

04) Place a piece of clay in the center of the cardboard and stick the tip of the pencil into the clay.

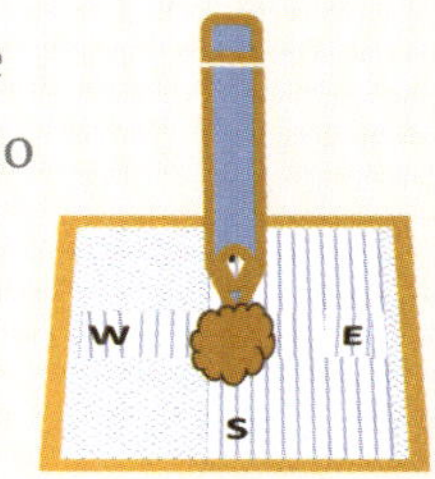

05) Use a pin to fasten the straw to the top of the eraser. Make sure it's centered. You may also want to wiggle the pin back-and-forth a bit to make sure the arrow can spin easily.

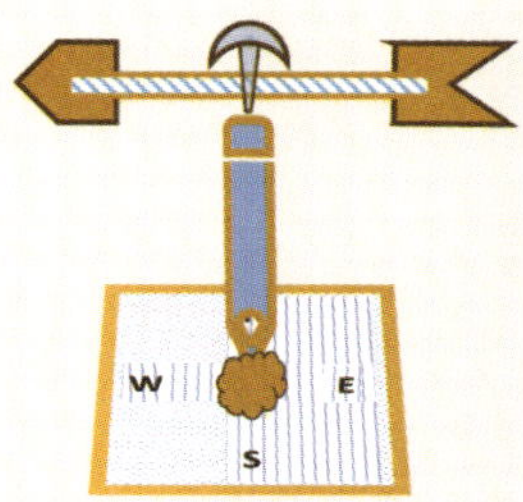

Now observe! The arrow will point in the direction the wind is blowing.

Rajeshwari Chatterjee

(1922–2010)

Engineer

A young girl on a ship; a voyage about to commence,
as her country stood thirty days from independence.

The scene was electric,
the future seemed near.
As she sailed to Michigan,
to become an engineer.

Microwaves and radio waves were no cause for worry,
to this mistress of electricity, intrepid Rajeshwari!

Do well at school. Focus on physics. Complete B.Sc and M.Sc from Bangalore. And go to Michigan University, USA, to study electrical engineering. Sounds like the plan of a young millennial, right? Wrong! This is what Rajeshwari Chatterjee, born nearly a century ago in 1922, accomplished.

Rajeshwari, whose grandmother Kamalamma Dasappa, was one of the earliest women graduates of India, was a pioneering Indian lady in the field of electrical engineering. She started her brilliant academic journey in a school in Bangalore. The school had been set up by her own grandmother in Basavanagudi, Bangalore (Basavanagudi also contributed a part of its name to the famous, but imaginary town, Malgudi in R.K. Narayan's brilliant books). Rajeshwari continued her studies in Central College, Bangalore and focused on physics and mathematics.

Showing glimpses of her enormous acumen, she topped her university, securing first rank. She won many accolades for her academic achievements – the Mummadi Krishnaraja Wodeyar Award, the MT Narayan Iyengar Prize and the Walters Memorial Prize.
On completion of her master's in 1943, she joined the Indian Institute of Science, Bangalore, as a research student.

At a time when India was on the cusp of winning her freedom and embarking on a fresh journey, Rajeshwari emulated her nation's trajectory, receiving a scholarship from the interim Indian Government to go to the USA and study electrical engineering at Michigan University, Ann Arbor. She left India in July 1947, just before India's independence. Not only was this a pioneering move, but even the physical journey was long and arduous – it took Rajeshwari 30 days to reach the USA from

India by sea. In Michigan University, she completed her Master's degree from the Department of Electrical Engineering. She subsequently underwent training at the National Bureau of Standards in Washington. Returning to Michigan in 1949, she completed her PhD in 1953.

On completion of her PhD, Rajeshwari returned to India, to become a faculty member at the Indian Institute of Science, teaching electromagnetic theory, microwave technology and radio engineering to budding students.

She was the only female faculty member in the institute.

Bringing her personal life and professional life closer, she married her colleague and fellow faculty member Sisir Kumar Chatterjee. She set up a research laboratory, along with her husband, to conduct research on microwave engineering.

Rajeshwari went on to become the Chairperson of the Department of Electrical Communication Engineering. And eventually retired in 1982. Even after retiring from active work, Rajeshwari continued to mentor students and promote education for women in the field of science. She also authored many books – in subjects as diverse as engineering and personal history. Her daughter followed in her footsteps becoming a professor of electrical and bio-medical engineering at the University of Nevada, USA.

Though Rajeshwari passed away in 2010, her work and personal journey continue to be an inspiration for many women seeking the path of science.

So, you want to be an Engineer

That's great.

Have you heard of Leonardo da Vinci.

Yes, he is a famous artist who drew 'Mona Lisa' and the 'Last Supper'. But did you know that he was also a prodigal engineer. He is credited with having made designs which no one could think of at that time. He designed an arch bridge for the Sultan of the Ottoman Empire.

Although it was not built at the time, centuries later in 2001, a bridge was built in Norway using the same design. Another idea that Da Vinci is credited with is gated canals. The design is like modern canals such as the famous Panama Canal. So, if you become an engineer, you'd be like Leonardo da Vinci. Now that's cool, right?

Activity

Create a circuit

This activity has been amended to make do with a common ingredient found in every kitchen. A custom art would be created for the book on the theme of 'Gutsy Girls of Indian Science'.

Supplies

- 2 pieces of chart paper (any size)
- 5 mm aluminium strip
(cut from aluminium foil found in the kitchen)
- 1 3V coin-cell battery
- 1 LED light (3-4 mm – any colour)
- Crayons, markers, coloured pencils or paint
- Decorative items for greeting card (optional)
- Clear tape
- Pencil
- Scissors
- Binder clip

Directions

01) Fold one piece of chart paper in half so that it resembles a greeting card.

02) Fold the second piece of chart paper to match the first, then set it aside for later.

03) Decorate the front of your card, identifying a place to add an LED light.

04) Using the pencil or scissors, carefully poke a small hole in the folded card for your LED light.

05) Insert the LED from the back of the card and bend the wires out so it doesn't fall through.

06) In a corner of the card, mark a place for the coin-cell battery.

07) On the back of the card, use the pencil to draw out the circuit you want to make so that a line runs from each LED leg to the battery. The battery has a plus (positive terminal) or minus (negative terminal) symbol on each side. The LED also has positive and negative terminals – the longer leg is positive (anode) and the shorter one is negative (cathode).

08) To make the LED light up, you need to connect the negative side of the battery to the negative leg of the LED and the positive side of the battery to the positive leg of the LED.

Create a circuit

01 Tape down your aluminium strip over the lines you drew, carefully folding the tape to "turn" any corners.

02 Using clear tape, secure the legs of the LED so that they are on top of the aluminium tape.

03 Place the battery in its designated spot on the circuit and fold the corner so that each line of aluminium strip contacts the appropriate terminal of the battery. Secure with a binder clip when you want to keep the LED on.

04 If you want to write a message on the interior of the card, use the second folded card piece to cover the circuit. Secure it with a glue stick and write your message. Be sure to leave access to the corner with the battery.

What's happening?

Electricity can only travel through certain conductive materials. When the aluminium metal tape connects the battery, LED and back to the battery, a circuit is completed. Electricity flows from the battery to light up the LED. What happens if you try to add more LED lights?

Raman Parimala

(1948-Present)

Mathematician

Can you guess a subject that divides
students into two opposite sides?

Maths is either your joy, your pride,
or it makes you run and hide!
Love it or hate it, you can't ignore the fact,
that without Maths one can't attack...
the world's problems big and small!

So, do embrace it if you hear the call of science;
for it's a field rather specific,
and maths will help you become terrific.
Well, who knows, you might even wax poetic
about equations, geometry and arithmetic?
Go on, you could do us proud, kid,
just the way Raman Parimala did!

India has produced some legendary mathematicians and is credited with the discovery of the 'zero'. However, most of these mathematicians were men and it is only in recent decades that women have received their due credit in this field.

Raman Parimala is one such illustrious example who has become an inspiration for girls who love maths.

Born on November 21, 1948, in Mayiladuthurai, Nagapattinam district of Tamil Nadu in an educated and progressive family, Raman Dummi Parimala had a great environment that kindled a love for learning. Her biggest support came from her father. He was a Professor of English Literature and when Raman showed an interest in pursuing maths, he ensured that she received the best education.

Growing up in Chennai, she completed her schooling and went on to study at the prestigious Stella Maris college. Her long association with mathematics started early and took her to many famous educational institutions. The list of institutions with which Parimala was associated—either as a student, or an academician—is long and impressive. She completed her master's from Madras University and her PhD from Bombay University. She subsequently taught at Tata Institute of Fundamental Research. Later she held positions at the Swiss Federal Institute of Technology in Zurich and the University of Lausanne in Switzerland. She was also associated with University of California, Berkeley, University of Chicago, Ohio State University and the Paris-Sud University, Orsay.

In 2005, Raman became a Professor of Mathematics at the Emory University in Atlanta, Georgia. Raman's main work has been in the field of algebra in mathematics. One of her early works was publishing the first example of nontrivial quadratic space in an affine plane. Over time she worked on either supporting or refuting many mathematical conjectures. In the study of mathematics, an idea or a proposition that is generally assumed to be true, and is supported by evidence, but which has not been conclusively proven to be true by an irrefutable proof, is called a conjecture. There are many mathematical conjectures, which attract the attention of academicians who try to either prove them to be correct or prove them to be false.

Raman worked on quadratic forms leading to the study of real algebraic geometry, complex algebraic geometry and cohomology theories. Based on her studies and investigations, she published elegant papers either supporting or refuting many conjectures. Her work on Serre's conjecture, led to her winning the 2005 prize in mathematics from the Third World Academy of Sciences.

But this is not all. Parimala has many such achievements to her name. She is a fellow of Indian Academy of Science, the Indian National Science Academy and the American Mathematical Society. She was invited as a speaker at the International Congress of Mathematics, twice, in 1994 and 2010. The ICM is held once every four years and to be invited as a speaker is considered a great honour and a reflection of outstanding achievement in the field of mathematics.

She is also the recipient of the Shanti Swaroop Bhatnagar Award, the highest scientific award in India.

Throughout her journey as a phenomenal mathematician Raman has remained focused on teaching. Talking about teaching as a professor at the Emory University she said, 'I've always enjoyed teaching. It's fun to work with undergraduate students. They are so enthusiastic.'

Raman had great support from her teachers and her husband. Her teachers at Stella Maris insisted that she should not take up a teaching position at the same college because she displayed the brilliance needed for a research career. When Raman got married, she moved abroad with her husband to Dar-es-Salaam in Tanzania. When her husband realized that Parimala's career prospects in Tanzania weren't bright, he quit his job, and was ready to go with her to a more suitable place. Raman joined ETH, University of Lausanne, Zurich, Switzerland, for her postdoctoral research. This was a pivotal experience that set Raman up for a great future in her field.

Raman's own enthusiasm for mathematics, her love for teaching and her many accomplishments will continue to inspire many young students to chart out a path in the field of mathematics.

So, you want to be a *Mathematician*

That's great. But which one? Did you think that maths is just some arithmetic and algebra?

Maths is a vast field made up of many areas of study. Topology is the study of geometric objects under continuous deformations. Actuarial science is the study of financial risk using mathematical models. Combinatorics is the field of mathematics that is about counting. Game theory, which sounds fun, is a branch of mathematics that analyses competitive strategies. So, you have many, many, options to choose from when you become a mathematician.

Activity

Möbius strip

Ever since the German mathematician August Möbius discovered it in 1858, the möbius strip has fascinated the world. It has triggered the development of an entire branch of mathematics called topology. What makes this shape special? Imagine an ant walking on the strip in a straight line. It would make a trip around the strip without changing sides because there is no edge on this surface. This is an example of a non-orientable object and is a simple physical illustration of this property. It's a good example of the non-intuitive thinking that higher level maths deals with.

Where have you seen this shape in real life? The recycle symbol on waste bins and product packaging is a möbius strip too.

Instructions

01) Cut out a thin rectangular strip of paper and label the corners.

02) Now, fold the paper with a half turn and bring the corresponding sides to face each other.

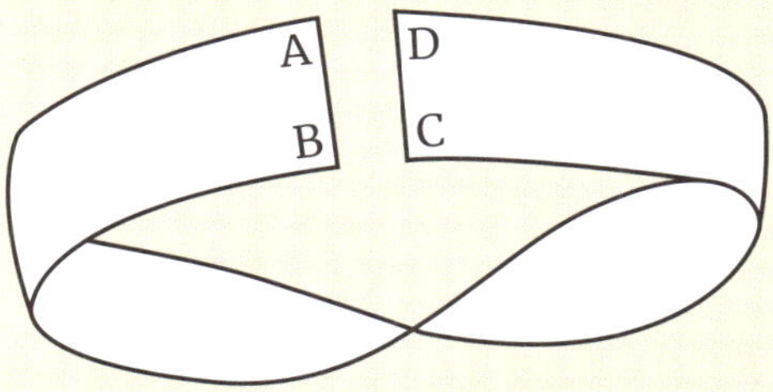

03) Finally, glue the two ends together. Your Möbius strip is ready!

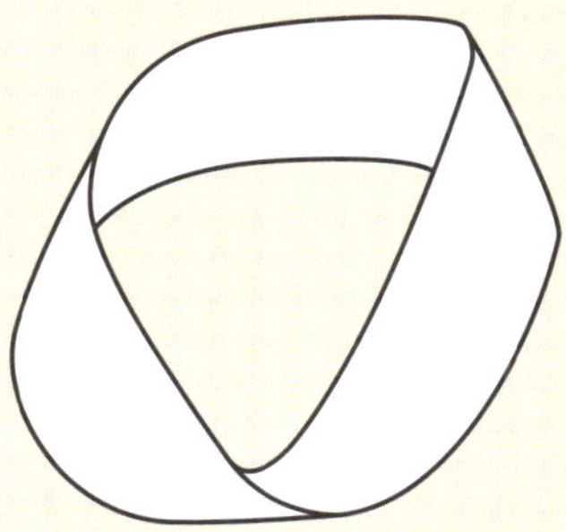

Bibha Chowdhuri

(1913–1991)

Physicist

What's in a name, you might ask?
Why does it matter, what's its task?
Can a little baby's moniker,
tell us something regarding her?
Ever so often it predicts,
a life's tune, its lyrics.

**The leading lady of Physics,
the aptly named Bibha –
– was so brilliant by far,
that this scientist exemplar
lent her name to a cosmic star!**

When a baby girl was born in 1913 in Kolkata in the home of a well-educated zamindar (landowner) family, her parents decided to name her Bibha.

Bibha in Sanskrit means 'brightness', and the little girl lived up to her name, encouraged by the supportive environment at home.

The family was related to the famous Indian scientist Sir Jagdish Chandra Bose and held views that were ahead of their time. One such view was that both men and women should be educated. It may seem unthinkable now but most Indian girls at the time were not sent to school and female literacy was very low in British India. Bibha's mother, Urmila Devi made sure that her four daughters and son received a good education.

Bibha went to one of the oldest colleges in India (and Asia) – the Bethune College in Kolkata. She went on to complete her B.Sc degree with honours in physics and was the only woman in her batch to complete her M.Sc. in physics from the University of Calcutta in 1936. She was 23 years old at that time. She led a simple life and was immersed in her books and research work. She requested Dr. Debendra Mohan Bose, a relative of her mother's, for permission to join his research group on subatomic particles. Dr. Debendra Bose was the nephew of Sir JC Bose and would go on to become the Director of the Bose Institute of Kolkata. Although Bibha was a relative, Dr. Bose was not sure whether the projects he worked on could be done by a woman. He finally relented and Bibha went on to publish three papers in collaboration with Dr. Bose in the esteemed international journal 'Nature'.

Bibha's work on particle physics was pathbreaking. She developed a new method of studying high energy particles using photographic plates. For the experiment, she took the half–tone plates to a mountainous region in West Bengal and exposed them to cosmic rays. Unlike now, no particle accelerators existed in her time, so the only way to access these particles to study them was through cosmic rays. She examined these plates under the microscope to check for tell-tale unique marks left by particles. She then compared them to a control set of plates that had been exposed to known particles with predictable marks. She was able to find two new particles – the pi-masons or pions and the mu-mesons or muons. There had been speculation that these two particles existed but no definitive proof existed till Bibha and Dr. Bose published their findings. Bibha also calculated the mass of these particles relative to the mass of an electron. Soon after, World War II started, and it became hard to get the plates and other equipment needed to continue these experiments.

Seven years later, the Nobel Prize was won by British Physicist Dr. Cecil Frank Powell, "for his development of the photographic method of studying nuclear processes and his discoveries regarding mesons made with this method". He was elected a Fellow of the Royal Society (FRS). He later wrote a book in which he mentioned Bibha and Bose's work.

Bibha moved to England in 1945 to work on her doctorate with Sir Patrick Blackett as her advisor. The subject of her research here was air showers. When high energy particles from space enter the atmosphere, they bump into the nucleus of matter in our atmosphere. This causes subatomic particles to be released in a shower. Bibha used a device invented by Sir

Patrick for her experiments. She submitted her thesis in 1949 and earned her doctorate in 1952. Sir Patrick went on to win a Nobel Prize for his work on cosmic rays and the invention of the device used by Bibha – the cloud chamber. Did Bibha's research contribute to his observations and discoveries? Not enough is known to answer that question.

Dr. Bibha returned to India in 1949 and became the first woman scientist to work at the prestigious Tata Institute of Fundamental Research. Dr Homi J. Bhabha recruited her since he was working on cosmic rays too. After TIFR, she worked at the Bengal Engineering College in Kolkata. Next, she worked at the Research Laboratory (PRL) in Ahmedabad when it was headed by Dr. Vikram Sarabhai. She was involved in the Kolar Gold Field (KGF) experiments. Her last research paper was published in 1990, a year before her death at the age of 78. She had chosen not to marry.

Although, Bibha's colleagues went on to win many honours, prizes and accolades, she went largely unrecognized in her lifetime.

She had said in an interview, "it is a tragedy that we have so few women physicists today".

It is only now that her story is getting told, thanks largely due to the research by Rajinder Singh and Suprakash C. Roy who undertook the task of rediscovering her. Things are better for women scientists today.

Recently, the IAU has renamed the star HD 86081 as Bibha. She continues to shine and inspire young girls who would like to be scientists too.

So, you want to be a Physicist

To answer that, you might want to first understand why it is useful to study physics. It is very hard to define exactly what is studied under physics. That's because our understanding of the subject is evolving so quickly that the definitions most often speak of the past rather than what's at the frontier of this science.

Still, it would be useful to consider physics as the branch of science that studies the nature and properties of matter and energy in reference to space and time and how they are related to each other.

Physicists make sense of what goes on around us, not just on our planet but also on a cosmic scale. Some of the most famous and well-liked scientists who have captured the imagination of people across centuries have been physicists. Aristotle, Sir Isaac Newton and Albert Einstein were all trying to unravel the mysteries of this science in their own way. Physics as a science could do with more women in the field. Do you want to know more about this subject? Here's an activity for you:

Activity

Think of an area or topic within physics which you find interesting. It could be the composition of our Universe, the speed of supersonic airplanes, the path taken by particles inside fluids, the behaviour of quarks – absolutely anything you like. Now, find out the names of some famous physicists who have been instrumental in our understanding of your topic of choice. Learn more about their lives, their contributions, the challenges they faced, and the role played by their discovery in changing how we see our world.

Do you think you might like doing similar work? Look for more examples and study them to decide whether it is something you would like to pursue. The world is waiting!

Star Gazing

Cut out the template, fold it into a cube and add holes with a needle where there are stars! Add your little LED (candle) light and close the box! You are ready to go star gazing!

Scan the QR code to print the image below.

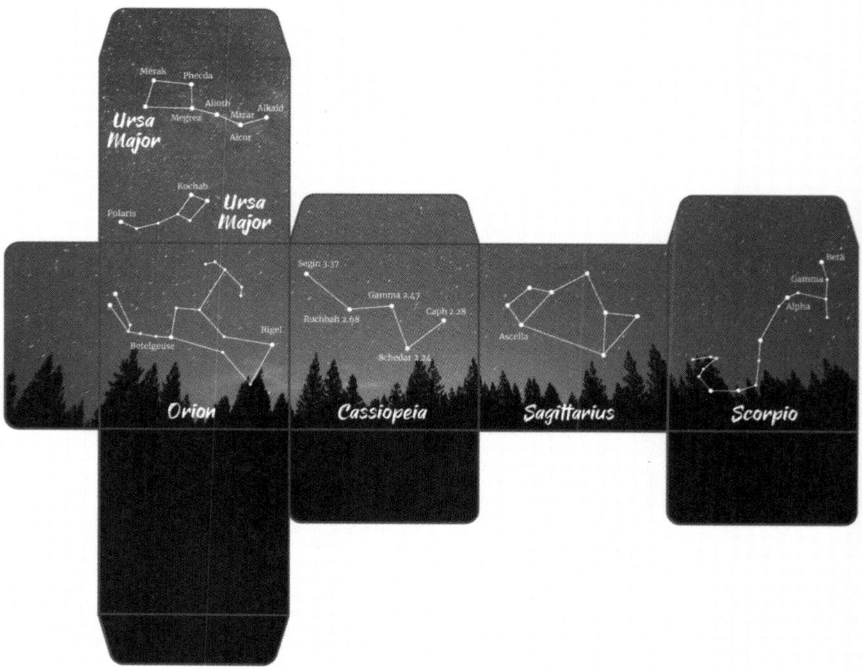

Kamal Ranadive

(1917–2001)

Medicine

Kamal was a lady who could juggle
several roles without much trouble.

Her day job was a life enhancer,
after all, she found a cure for cancer.

Yet, as we peel away this layer,
we find the patriarchy slayer.

Rallying women scientists together
to shake off the chains that tether.

And weigh them down when they try
to flap their wings and fly to the sky!

Most parents wish a great life for their children and their dreams reflect this desire. But it's only a few who can have dreams that transcend the social bounds of the time. In the case of Kamal, her father wanted her to become a doctor. While it doesn't sound like a pathbreaking thought in the 21st century, nearly a hundred years back this was largely unthinkable. However, sometimes life has an even better plan, and Kamal embarked on a journey that possibly led to her impacting and saving lives in a way no one could have imagined.

Kamal was fortunate to have been born in the early 1900s in a very progressive family that valued education much more than societal norms of the time. Her father Dinakar was a biology professor in Fergusson College in Pune. Consequently, she studied at the best girls' school in Pune, and went on to finish school with excellent grades. While her father had wished for her to pursue medicine and become a doctor, Kamal chose to chart her own path and decided to pursue botany and zoology at Fergusson College. Perhaps this independent-minded approach was just a natural result of the high level of scientific intellect that eventually made her one of the leading lights in her chosen field.

After graduation, Kamal completed her post-graduation in cytogenetics from the College of Agriculture, Pune. Remember that this was 1943! At that time, there were only a handful of Indians who were pursuing education in higher sciences, and the women were even fewer. But if graduation and post-graduation were a great achievement for most people in her time, for Kamal Ranadive, these were just the initial milestones in her impressive journey as a pioneering scientist. She relocated to Bombay (now known as Mumbai) for her doctoral research under a brilliant guide – Dr. Khanolkar.

Dr. Khanolkar was the founder of the Indian Cancer Research Institute.

In 1949, Kamal completed her doctorate and was now rewarded by being officially referred to as Dr. Kamal Ranadive. On Dr. Khanolkar's encouragement, she decided to continue her pursuit of scientific research and education in the form of post-doctoral research.

She secured a research fellowship at the prestigious John Hopkins University in New York, USA. Not just that, she also got the opportunity, while at the John Hopkins University, to assist Dr. George Otto Gey. Dr. Gey was a biologist who did pioneering work on HeLa cell line. (This cell line is credited with having helped in the future development of polio vaccines, the first human clone and in vitro fertilization.)

This was a time when many bright Indian scientists had gone to the west, especially to the USA, since the facilities and environment for scientific research were much better in the developed western countries compared to India, which was still struggling to provide a better living standard for its people after independence and the end of colonial rule. Not surprisingly, many such scientists opted to stay in the western countries and pursue the work in their chosen field. Kamal too had the same option, but she chose to return to India and contribute to developing the research capabilities in her country. After returning to India, she joined the ICRC as a Senior Research Fellow and eventually served, between 1966 and 1970, as the director of the institute founded by her one-time mentor Dr. Khanolkar. During her research work, Dr. Kamal made many contributions that furthered the work in the field of cancer research and medicine. Her pioneering work on studying cancer through animal models helped generate insights into the origin of leukaemia, breast cancer and oesophageal cancer.

She helped discover the update for the leprosy vaccine in India.

She also proved the relation between cancer and the interactions between hormones and the tumour virus.

Her contribution to science was not limited to the laboratory and research. Dr. Kamal understood the challenge of bringing in and retaining women talent in the world of STEM. To encourage more women to enter the field of science, she along with a few of her colleagues, founded the Indian Women Scientists' Association in 1973. Today this institute, with multiple branches all over India, provides hostel and day care facilities to enable women to pursue their interest in science.

Dr. Kamal contributed towards the development of science in a way that is difficult to emulate. She did pioneering research in the field of cancer, chose to do her work in India in a more challenging environment rather than the comfort of foreign institutes, tried hard to bridge the challenges that plagued the entry of women into the field of science, and worked amongst the tribals of Maharashtra to address malnutrition issues among women and children. No surprise then that she received the Padma Bhushan in 1982, one of the highest civilian honours in India, for her extraordinary contribution. Even though Dr. Kamal Ranadive passed away in 2001, the story of her life's journey and accomplishments continues to inspire many women scientists as it does to promote science in India, the way she did during her lifetime.

So, you want to find a cure for *Cancer*

Cancer is one of the most dreaded diseases known to us. It cuts across all barriers of race, age and gender.

The battle against cancer and other diseases is far from over. And when, occasionally, a new disease like Covid–19 emerges, intense, concerted teamwork by scientists is needed to create vaccines against it. Medicine is one of the fields where a young scientist like yourself can have the largest positive impact on humanity. Are biology and chemistry subjects that interest you? If yes, then you could consider a career in medicine.

Activity

Did you know that the plants around us yield compounds that are active ingredients in medicines?

Walk into your kitchen and pick up a pinch of the yellow turmeric powder in your spice box. Do you know the name of the powerful compound in turmeric that has made it very interesting to scientists?

Curcumin, the main active ingredient, is a very strong antioxidant and has anti-inflammatory properties.

01) It is being researched for its potential role in fighting several diseases including cancer.
Its molecule is represented like this:

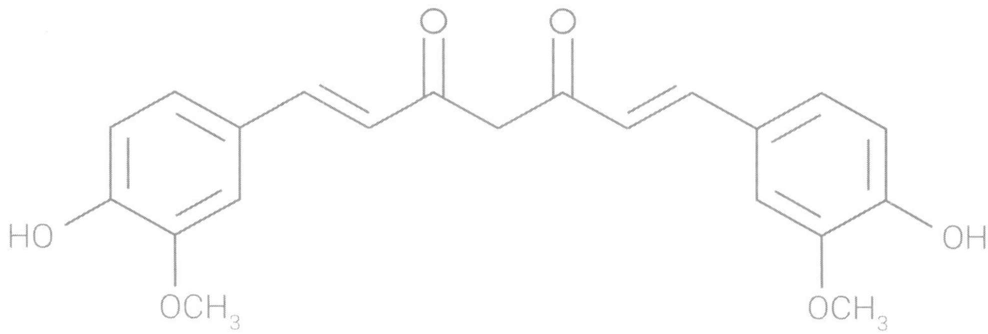

The curcumin content of turmeric is not high – it is around 3% by weight.

02) Also, it is not readily absorbed in the bloodstream. It is for this reason that medicinal supplements of curcumin are designed to increase the bioavailability of this active ingredient. Also, here's a fun fact – it helps to consume curcumin with black pepper because the compound piperine found in the pepper enhances the absorption of curcumin by 2000%.

03) Finally, curcumin is fat soluble. That's probably the reason it was traditionally consumed in India as part of dishes tempered in oil or consumed with milk which has fat content of its own.

Spice Game

Here's a fun way for you to find out what health benefits the other spices in your kitchen can provide. Cut out the four circles and carefully cut along the dotted lines while keeping the central circles intact.

Benefits

Cut out the circle and cut along the dotted line ensuring the inner circle remains intact. Write the benefits from the "answers" given.

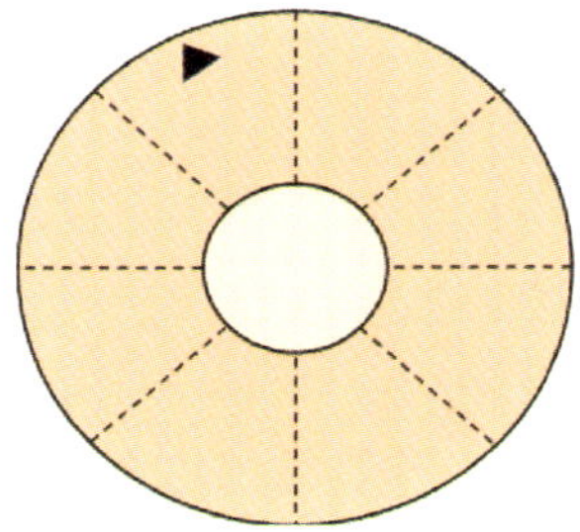

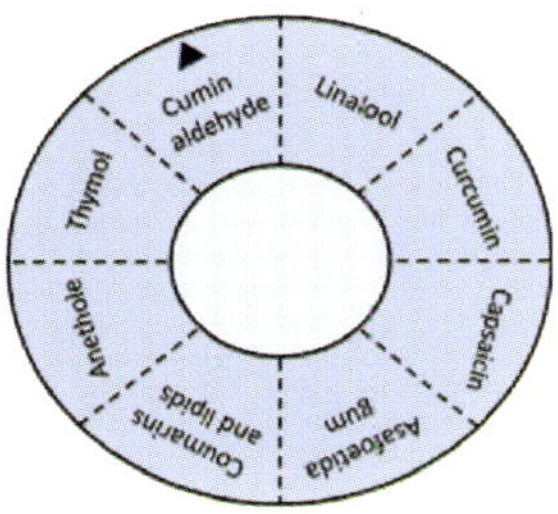

Active Ingredient

Write down the benefits of the corresponding spices and cut the circles as specified.

Name of Spice

Cut out the circle and cut along the dotted line ensuring the inner circle remains intact.

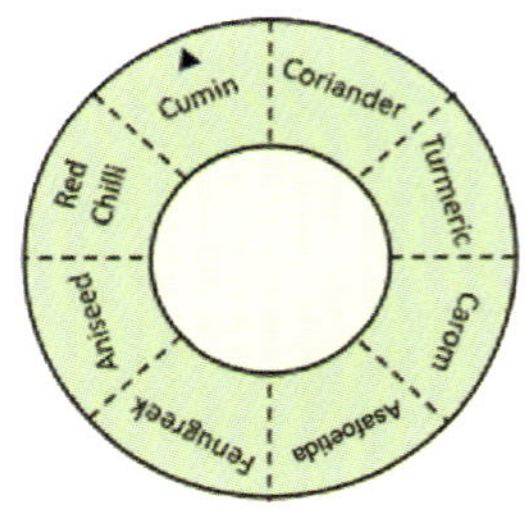

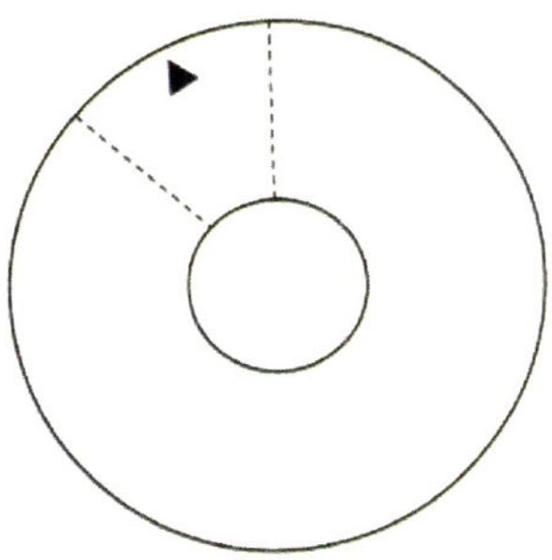

Cover Page

Cut out the circle and the window ensuring that the inner circle remains intact. Decorate the rest of the circle as you wish.

Place the circles in this order with the arrows aligned. Finally, place the biggest circle which you decorated on top of these and carefully put a pin through the centre. You can teach your friends about your spice medicines now!

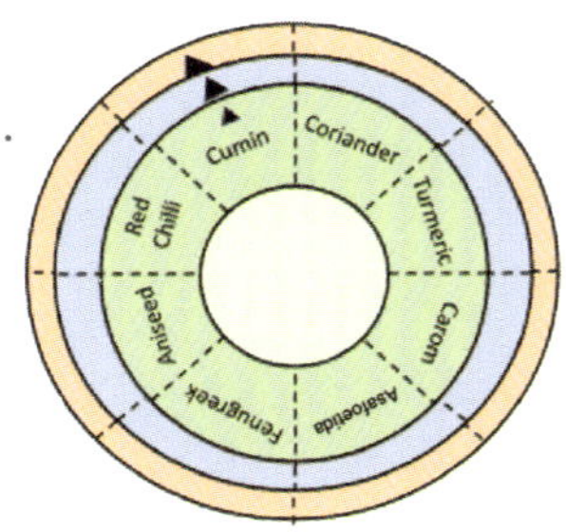

Answers for the Benefit Circle

01 Cumin-cumin aldehyde – contains antioxidants, is anticancer, treats diarrhoea, is anti-inflammatory, lowers cholesterol.

02 Coriander- linalool, alpha-pinene – is anti-inflammatory and antiviral

03 Turmeric - curcumin – is anti-inflammatory, a painkiller, antiseptic, combats arthritis

04 Red Chilli- capsaicin – increases metabolism, is a painkiller, reduces insulin spikes

05 Asafoetida- asafoetida gum – helps in digestion, weight loss, controls diabetes, fights respiratory problems and infections

06 Fenugreek- coumarins and lipids – reduces risk of diabetes, is anti-inflammatory, a painkiller

07 Aniseed- anethole – used to treat colic, indigestion, stomach-aches, and stomach cramps

08 Carom-thymol oil – treats digestive problems, also has antifungal and antibacterial properties

Scan the QR code to print this activity.

Ilina Singh

Ilina is young, curious and believes she can make the world a better place by solving problems big and small. She thinks of herself as an artist who loves science. Or is it the other way round? She used to scribble on all the walls she could reach as a young child. And opened electronic gadgets to "see what's inside". Leonardo da Vinci, Einstein and Steve Jobs among many others discovered their gifts at the intersection of their left and right brains and Ilina believes we can all find better outcomes if we allow our complete set of abilities to shine.

Last year, as Ilina sat down to select her subjects for high school, she investigated what she could expect in the future as a young scientist. She and her friends had not heard of any notable woman scientist except Marie Curie so she was quite surprised to come across a tweet from the Government of India celebrating eleven Indian women scientists. As she read their life stories, she was really convinced that more girls needed to know that such brave and intelligent women had paved the way for future generations.

She started by painting their portraits and sending them to the Prime Minister on Republic Day, expressing her desire to tell young boys and girls about their stellar stories. This got her a very encouraging reply. She also met the author of the tweet that had inspired her—Ms. Smriti Irani—and got a heartening response to the idea of writing a book on these trailblazers.

Ilina discovered that the UNESCO had worked extensively in the field of women in STEM. She sought the guidance of the team led by Mr. Eric Falt and they were very generous with their time and mentorship. The team at HarperCollins – Ananth and Tina – were believers and collaborators in the idea and helped make the dream come true.

It is Ilina's wish that girls and boys see science and maths as equally interesting ways to explore and understand our world and leave it better than we found it. Ilina lives in Gurgaon with her parents and her dearest dog Uzi.